A–Z OF CREWE

Places - People - History

Paul Hurley

Acknowledgements

I would like to thank historian Jules Hornbrook for his valued help with the local history of the town and for allowing me to use photos from his archive; Maria Mulliner of Morning Foods (Mornflake) for providing the photo of the family; the editor of the *Sainsbury Magazine* for allowing me to use their Mornflake article. Some of the old images are courtesy of Cheshire Archives and Local Studies, and I thank Katie Owen for her help. Thanks to Melissa and Debbie from the Lakemore Farm park and Geoff Wilde for his information regarding Sir Hardman Earl and Mersey Vale; Nick Grant of Amberley Publishing for his advice and guidance; Phil Braithwaite for allowing me to use the rail photos; Ed Whitby of Whitby Morrison for his valued help and advice; and, of course, as usual, my wife Rose for her patience and valued help during the writing of the book.

First published 2019

Amberley Publishing
The Hill, Stroud, Gloucestershire, GL5 4EP
www.amberley-books.com

ISBN 978 1 4456 9507 5 (print)
ISBN 978 1 4456 9508 2 (ebook)

British Library Cataloguing in Publication Data.
A catalogue record for this book is available from the British Library.

Origination by Amberley Publishing.
Printed in Great Britain.

Contents

Introduction

This will be my first book solely featuring Crewe, although a mention did appear in my *Cheshire Through Time* and *Brewing in Cheshire*. While researching this book, I soon found that unlike Nantwich, Crewe has been decimated and has a dearth of ancient properties. To see just how much has gone one only has to peruse the excellent *Crewe Through Time* by Peter Ollerhead. As with all of the Through Time books, it is easy to see what was there and what has now been swept away and Crewe has a lot to see. Row upon row of well-built terraced houses courtesy of the railway company were ruthlessly swept away in the early 1960s to build the new Crewe that resembles a town badly bombed in the war and rebuilt in the highly questionable way after building works were carried out in the '50s and '60s. Had the many well-built and sturdy terraced houses, which once housed the railway workers and were demolished, been brought up to date they could be providing valuable living accommodation.

Crewe is, in one way, completely unique due to the speed in which it appeared. The streets that were built by the railway company (in the order that they were built) were Delamere Street, Market Street (then called Coppenhall Street), Sandon Street, Prince Albert Street, Earle Street (originally called Small Lane), Liverpool Street, Manchester Street, Crewe Street, Church Street and onwards. The town and railway works continued to develop and grow, and in 1861 the new railway works were erected.

It is relevant at this stage to quote a popular magazine of the day, the *Illustrated London News*, dated 19 January 1861, when it reported that 'the great progress of the town had indeed been made in the first twenty years of its existence. What was a small village with a few farmhouses, now is a town of 1,500 dwellings, 9,000 inhabitants and possesses its church, chapels, Market Hall, Mechanics' Institute, Public Schools and a Municipal organisation. Truly a rapidly expanding New Town.'

So let's go back to 30 August 1930 and see what J. Cumming Walters said about it in his book *Romantic Cheshire*:

> A puny village called Crewe existed before steam locomotion was dreamt of; but the monsters came, breathed their hot breath into it, gave it tentacles, made it a roaring giant. Here we see lines winding, curving, bending, wriggling, starting suddenly for a new direction, losing themselves round such mysterious corners, joining, running side by side, widening, contracting – was there ever such intricacy all turned magically to use and order as at Crewe? There are spacious sheds like huge reservoirs in which leviathans spawn; for here come to shape and motion monsters that will roll, thud and scurry away and be lost rapidly in the distance.

I

Crewe was, and up to a point still is, a railway town. Firstly, let's see how that came about. Although Crewe was in the Domesday Book under the Welsh name of Creu, it was of no consequence until the railway arrived.

In 1831 a census was taken by Mr Richard Sherwin in Monks Coppenhall, who found that the hamlet soon to be part of Crewe contained eighty-one males and sixty-seven females. In 1851, just twenty years later, the population had increased to 4,491. Before the arrival of the Grand Junction Railway, there was no Crewe to speak of. As the railway system grew in magnitude, Crewe increased in population and importance, a significance that was worldwide. The population is in the region of 71,000.

The Grand Junction Railway (GJR) in 1840 had taken over the Liverpool & Manchester Railway and would soon become the London & North Western Railway (LNWR). It became quite evident in those early days that railways were more than a fad. The GJR committee decided that what it needed was a factory to manufacture railway locomotives and all of the other paraphernalia for this new transport system.

Edge Hill in Liverpool already had a railway facility, including Edge Hill station, the oldest passenger station in the world that is still in use today. It was from here that the Grand Junction recruited their first members of staff. In 1843 it was decided to move the works to a more central position. The first choice was Nantwich with its transport links to roads and canals, but when plans were underway to move from Edge Hill, the canal owners, forseeing the loss of business, fought it. They persuaded the people of Nantwich that the smoke from the GJR engines would harm them and their livestock. Even the agreed move from Edge Hill to Monks Coppenhall was contentious, but the location was ideal as it was within the Midland Gap and sat upon the heavy clay lands of central Cheshire, lands that were owned by Richard Edleston from Nantwich, a man who was in full agreement with the development of railways. The new GCR had already opened a station, or rather a halt, at Crewe on the Warrington/Birmingham line in 1837. By 1842 this halt became a hub with lines to Chester, Liverpool, Manchester, Shrewsbury and Stoke-on-Trent being added over the years. So the workshops were moved to Cheshire. In fact, it was not actually within Crewe until 1936 when the boundary of the town incorporated Church Coppenhall.

The area was sparsely inhabited, so to house the workers 220 cottages were built in the small village of Monks Coppenhall, which was soon to be incorporated into what was another small hamlet, called Crewe. It is here that what was to become the huge Crewe Railway Works was built. The first Superintendent of Crewe Works was Mr Francis F. Trevithick, the son of Mr Richard Trevithick, the inventor of the first railway engine. Not quite as famous as his father, Francis was required to resign in 1857 to make way for John Ramsbottom.

This new town was planned by the GJR's Engineer in Chief, Joseph Locke, in 1840, and by 1900 the works had a workforce of 10,146 persons. At the time there was strict rules of seniority and there were four classes of housing type. The senior managers were accommodated in large villas in their own expansive grounds, mainly in Chester

Street. Gothic-style houses were provided for middle management. Skilled workmen were accommodated in what were called 'blockhouses', where four families could be accommodated with a separate entrance for each one. Works foremen were housed in terraced housing in Victoria and Delamere Streets that became known as 'Gaffers Row'. Labourers were accommodated in terraced houses with four apartments in each. Most of the houses were demolished in the 1960s, but after public protest, some examples were preserved, but not the villas occupied by senior management, except the one featured in the book – we will look at the preserved ones later. In 1846 the GJR merged with the London & Birmingham Railway to form the London & North Western Railway (the LNWR), which, until 1923 when it became part of the London, Midland & Scottish Railway (the LMS), was the largest railway company in the world.

During the long life of the works, it would build some 7,000 steam locomotives and at its height employed 40.000 people. All of the requirements for the whole rail network were built or provided by the works, and by 1957 the works also built diesel locomotives. However, in 2005 it had less than 1,000 employees, and that figure has dropped even further now that the works are a shadow of its former self. Most of the works have now gone to make way for other things. So Crewe could arguably be called the birthplace of the railways in Britain and probably the world. Crewe station has also been a major hub and still is, and it is fair to say that at least in the early days as Crewe was being developed, it was being developed by the LNWR and the LNWR was Crewe!

A

Alexandra Stadium

Crewe Alexandra Football Club was named after either Princess Alexandra of Denmark, who married Queen Victoria's eldest son, later to be Edward VII, or the Alexandra pub, which was used by the railway workers and was a meeting place for the team. Before 1877 when the team formed a football club, they played cricket in the Earle Street ground. As railways are what Crewe is best known for, the nickname of the team is 'the Railwaymen' but is also called 'the Alex'. Coincidentally in 1877, the new Alexandra Recreation Ground was built with a cricket pitch, football pitch and cycling track, and the new team started to use it. At that time they were called the Alexandrians. In 1892 they were elected into the Second Division as one of the founding members, but failed to become professionals

The Alexandra football stadium in Gresty Road as it looks today.

so were not re-elected. At the same time, their lease on the recreation ground ended, and they spent some years sharing pitches and playing on fields until 1897. They then commenced playing at their new home in Gresty Road. The stadium was demolished to make way for new railway lines and rebuilt in 1906 to the west of the original site, where it is today. In the 1990s the stadium was completely rebuilt to a modern style. Most of the team's success was under Dario Gradi, who managed the club for twenty-four years, the longest-serving football manager at the time.

Atkins Technical Investigation Centre, Gresty Road

Included here is a typical railway building that is currently being used by the Atkins company as a technical investigation centre dealing with railway matters. The well-constructed building is typical of buildings built during the early days of the railways. Atkins is an important company that deals with various rail projects, infrastructure and planning, etc., worldwide.

Atkins Technical Investigation Centre, a typical railway building in Gresty Road.

B

Bentley Motors Limited

The company was formed in Cricklewood, London, in 1919 by W. O. Bentley.

Just five years later in 1924, a Bentley won the Le Mans twenty-four-hours race, which was followed up by wins in the race in 1927–30, and 2003! The early day wins were in the Bentley 4.5 litre and the Bentley Speed Six.

Walter Owen Bentley, known simply as W. O., started his career as a five-year premium apprentice with the Great Northern Railway at Doncaster. There he learned to design complex equipment for the railway. One quote from his railway days was that a single look at one of Stirling's 8 feet singles (locomotive) could move him profoundly. He was able to live out his childhood fantasy to actually drive a steam railway locomotive, namely one of the Great Northern's Atlantics. In fact, when he had completed his apprenticeship, he became a fireman on the main line expresses.

His longest day was when he shovelled 7 tons of coal on a none-stop run from Wakefield to London. In 1910 he completed his apprenticeship, but after his firing experience, he decided that the railways were not for him.

The front of what is now the Bentley Motors factory.

He became a motorcycle racer, competing in the Isle of Man TT twice on a Rex motorcycle. After an unsuccessful attempt as the Indian Team rider when a tyre burst on the first lap, he gave up that career and went back to college. He went to King's College and studied theoretical engineering, after which he took employment with National Motor Cab Company looking after their fleet of 250 Unic cabs.

In 1912 he teamed up with his brother Horace Milner Bentley and formed a company called Bentley and Bentley, specialising in selling the French Marque DFP (Doriot, Flandrin & Parant). In fact, W. O. raced a 2.5-litre tuned-up model 12/15 at Brooklands, breaking several records in 1913 and 1914.

Then the First World War started, and W. O. remembered the aluminium pistons that he had fitted in the DFP's that he raced. This he thought would be useful in aero engines for the war effort. He put this idea to the Royal Navy in the form of Commander Wilfrid Briggs, who was the liaison officer between the manufacturers and the navy. Cdr Briggs would be his senior officer when he was commissioned into the Royal Naval Air Service as an engineer. He visited the manufacturers, including Lord Hives of Rolls-Royce, and they designed their first aero engine with aluminium pistons, which was named The Eagle. He visited the Sunbeam factory and did likewise. The navy then gave him a team and the use of the Humber car factory to develop his own aeroplane engine. Here he designed the BR1 (Bentley Rotary1), later the BR2. After the war he was awarded the MBE and £8,000 from the Royal Commission on Awards to Inventors.

In 1919, he formed Bentley Motors Limited with his brother. They took on, or poached, engineers from other car companies and under the name Bentley Motors, they started work on designing a high-quality sports tourer.

The first Bentley 3 litre was delivered in 1921, which instantly gained widespread approval. After that, Bentley cars were raced in uphill trials and motor races including the Indianapolis 500. They entered the Le Mans twenty-four-hour races with Woolf (Babe) Barnato driving, who became the only driver to win all three races that he entered, gaining himself the nickname 'Bentley Boy'.

Soon Bentley started to get into financial difficulties and the directors blamed W. O. Woolf Barnato's grandfather was the famous South African diamond magnate Barney Barnato, whose heir was Woolf, and he inherited a vast fortune at a young age. So the Bentley company business assets were purchased by Woolf, and he became chairman. W. O. continued to work for the company but as an employee. It was against the advice of W. O. that Barnato authorised the design and building of a supercharged version of the 4.5-litre 'Blower' Bentley. It was built in premises away from the Bentley factory, and W. O. was not invited to participate. As he suspected, the durability of the 'Blower' Bentley was poor, and it failed on the track. Woolf continued to race Bentleys but the Great Depression came along, and in 1931 Bentley became a victim and went into liquidation. The company had accrued losses of £136,220. W. O., Woolf and another investor lost most of their money. Woolf, still being a bit astute, made a large investment in Rolls-Royce.

Napier & Son entered into negotiations to purchase Bentley, but they were beaten by Rolls-Royce. The Rolls-Royce company had inherited all of Bentley's assets, including

W. O. himself! The original Rolls-Royce plan was to use the Bentley name for cut-price versions of Rolls-Royce cars, but this was soon abandoned. W. O. believed, quite correctly, that Woolf had invested heavily in Rolls-Royce before the liquidation of Bentley and he was invited to become a director of the new subsidiary Bentley Motors (1931) Ltd.

W. O. then had an annus horriblis: his wife divorced him and he was ordered to return his works 8-litre Bentley. Luckily he was allowed by W. E. Rootes to test drive a new Hillman each weekend! He was obliged by the court to join Rolls-Royce at least from 1 May 1932 to the end of April 1935, during which time he was not treated well, being given jobs below his qualifications. The first new line of Bentleys came out of the Rolls-Royce factory and was promoted as 'The silent sports car'.

Once W. O. Bentley's contract ended, he worked for various firms designing cars. Firstly Lagonda during the Second World War, where he was employed in war work. In 1947 Lagonda was purchased by David Brown & Sons (Huddersfield) Ltd, who bought the company mainly to bring W. O. into their company. They already owned Aston Martin. Soon W. O. moved from Aston Martin-Lagonda to Armstrong Siddeley.

W. O. died on Friday 13 August 1971 aged eighty-two. He had been the patron of the Bentley Drivers' Club.

Bentley and Rolls-Royce moved to the old aero engine factory at Crewe, and in 1946 the first car off the production line was a Bentley MkVI.

The Bentley R Type was produced until 1955 and then came the Bentley S1/Rolls-Royce Silver Cloud. By now, the only real difference between the marks was the grill. Rolls Royce was for the moneyed gentry, and Bentley was in modern parlance 'cooler' slightly less quiet and faster.

The Rolls-Royce Motor Car Division was sold to Vickers in 1980, and Bentley changed it's image somewhat when they brought out the Bentley Mulsanne Turbo, which soon gained the nickname 'The Crewe Missile'.

In 1985 Bentley sales overtook Rolls-Royce sales for the first time since the business was moved to Crewe.

In 1998 the Bentley Arnage/Rolls-Royce Silver Seraph was the last of the dual-brand cars, and they were powered by a BMW Twin Turbo 4.5-litre engine. Also in 1998 Vickers announced that they were to sell the car division including the Crewe factory and Bentley, but not the Rolls-Royce Division, which would be known as Rolls-Royce in the event of a sale. It was sold to BMW and in 2000 was to be moved to a custom-built factory at Goodwood.

The Crewe factory and Bentley were purchased by Volkswagen, and the building of Bentley's continued. In 2003 the first independently built Bentley since the companies joined up in 1931 rolled off the line, and that was the Bentley Continental GT. When it was unveiled at the Pebble Beach Concourse d'Elegance in the USA, the Bentley Mulsanne was the first flagship car to be independently designed by Bentley Motors in nearly eighty years. Now Bentley is still the leading manufacturer of luxury cars and employs 4,000 people at it's Crewe factory in Pyms Lane.

One of the few remaining cottage rows built by the Grand Junction Railway.

Betley Street (Nos 1–19)

The first row of preserved houses that we come to. They were designed by John Cunningham for employees of the Grand Junction Railway in 1848, and are Grade II listed, as is the other side of the road – Nos 2–20. The GJR's engineer Joseph Locke had set out and planned the proposed new town of Crewe on behalf of the GJR. It was named after the nearby, albeit just over the border in Staffordshire, village of Betley. Also, in this particular area and built by the GJR, is Dorfold Street, named after the nearby Dorfold Hall and Tollitt Street, possibly named for the Tollet family, who resided at Betley Hall.

(St) Barnabas' Church

Built from 1884 to 1885 for the London & North Western Railway (LNWR) this church is near to its then workshops and was designed by Paley and Austin. It was consecrated on 20 October 1885, and the vicar was Revd W. C. Martin MA. It is in West Street and is still an active Anglican church. It was built in the Gothic Revival style and is a Grade II listed building. When built, it cost £4,000 (£400,000 today), and in 1886 it opened as St Barnabas' in Monks Coppenhall in the borough of Crewe.

St Barnabas' Church, one of the churches built for the LNWR.

Burma Star Island Memorial, a memorial to those who died in the Burma Campaign in Queens Park.

Burma Star Island Memorial

This unusually sited war memorial can be found by the lake at Queens Park in Crewe. It is known as the Burma Star Island and commemorates the memory of all who served in the Allied Forces in the South East Asia Command and who died during the Burma Campaign. It comprises a brass plaque mounted on a stone with an engraved inscription. Above the plaque is a replica of the Burma Star Medal. The memorial was unveiled by the Right Reverend G. A. Ellison DD, Bishop of Chester, on the 26 May 1968. It has been refurbished as part of the Queens Park lottery-funded renovation.

Beams, Hewitt Pearson Montague (1875–1948)

Born in Dublin in 1875 and educated in Ireland, he joined the LNWR at Crewe Works as a premium apprentice under Francis William Webb. On completion, he was made junior assistant to the works manager in 1899. In January of the following year, he

The inside of Crewe Works at the time when Hewitt Beams was responsible for upgrading the works.

was granted a leave of absence to join the armed forces in the South African War (the Boer War) attached to Paget's Horse until 1901, when he returned to his duties at Crewe. He accepted a few appointments until the outbreak of First World War when he was the personal assistant to the CME, C. J. Bowen-Cooke. He joined the army again on active service in the Royal Engineers Railway Company in which he travelled to France as part of the British Expeditionary Force.

He was, however, soon recalled to Crewe Works to take up the appointment as chief assistant and works manager with the responsibility for munitions and to prepare locomotives that were required overseas for the war effort. At the end of the war, from June 1919 until November 1920 he was deputy chief mechanical engineer of the LNWR. On the premature death of Bowen-Cooke, he became interim CME until 1 January 1922. At this time the LNWR combined with the Lancashire & Yorkshire Railway and his short spell as CME ended. He became the divisional engineer, Western Division, under George Hughes, the CME of the L&YR. This was a bad decision as Hughes was by then sixty-seven years old and the job should have gone to Beams. Shortly after the London, Midland & Scottish Railway (LMS) came into being, amalgamating the LNER and others. Beams became the mechanical engineer under the new regime and deputy CME under Ernest Lemon, who was CME of the LMS. He was passed over for promotion for the fourth time, William Stanier taking over from Lemon, and he resigned from his post on the 30 September 1934.

He had much success at Crewe, being responsible for the upgrading and modernisation of the works. Even when under the LMSR as deputy to Ernest Lemon, when the posts of CME was based at Derby, Beames remained at his house in Chester Place, Crewe, the official residence of the Crewe Works CME.

He remained as deputy to William Stanier until his retirement in 1934 at the age of fifty-nine.

He then took an interest in politics and became the chairman of the Cheshire County Council. In those days the council met in the LNWR-owned Crewe Arms Hotel in Crewe. He was also president of the Webbs Orphanage for several years and the Crewe Mechanics Institute. Beams received the CBE from the king in the 1946 Honours List for services as chairman of the Emergency Committee, County of Cheshire. H. P. M. Beams died on the 5 March 1948, aged seventy-two.

His son Peter Hewitt Beeston Beams was killed at Dunkirk as a second lieutenant in the Dragoon Guards. He is buried in the Tobruk War Cemetary. A memorial window was placed in Christ Church, Crewe, but as that window, like most of the church, has been knocked down it is in storage awaiting a suitable location.

Bombardier Railway Company

As previously mentioned, in 1840 the Grand Junction Railway set up a works and construction facility in Crewe. They were originally at Edge Hill in Liverpool during their operational period between 1845 and 1958. Under the Grand Junction Railway, the London & North Western Railway and the London, Midland & Scottish Railway over 7,000 steam railway locomotives and later diesel and electric locomotives were also built here. In 1969/70 the works were acquired by British Rail Engineering and became a BREL Workshop. They were engaged in the construction of new trains until 1989 when BREL was privatised and partly sold to a consortium comprising the international ABB Group, Trafalgar House and Employees.

Two years later the manufacture of new trains came to an end and the site was used as the vehicle and component repair centre.

The following year ABB obtained 100 per cent control of BREL Ltd and became ABB Transportation. In 1996 ABB and Daimler Benz combined to form Adtranz.

Finally, in 2001, the site was acquired by Bombardier Transportation UK Ltd. A great deal of downsizing had taken place in the mid-1980s. Bombardier carried out re-engineering and overhaul of railway bogies, wheels and traction at their Bombardier Services Site, Crewe Heavy Maintenance facility, in West Street, Crewe. Recently several parcels of land have been sold for development.

The entrance to what was one of the entrances to Crewe Works, now the Bombardier Company.

Crewe Works Joiner's Shop

The photo of the wood storage outside the joiner's shop at Crewe Works around 1910 gives an indication of the amount of work undertaken at the works. At this time virtually everything that the railways needed was made in house. Carriage building had already been moved to another works, Railway Town, Wolverton near Milton Keynes, who took on the job of building carriages including the ones for the Royal family. The manufacture of locomotives there had already been transferred to Crewe Works.

The stockpile of wood outside the Crewe Works joiner's shop.

Charles Bowen-Cooke (1859–1920)

Charles Bowen-Cooke was born at Orton Longueville in Huntingdonshire in 1859. In 1875 he became a premium apprentice and a pupil of Mr F. W. Webb. On completion of his training, he accepted a few appointments, later becoming assistant to Mr G. Whale when the latter became CME of Crewe Works, and Bowen-Cooke became superintendent of the Running Department of the Southern Division of the LNWR. When Mr Whale resigned in 1909, he became CME of Crewe Works. He was in charge at Crewe through the First World War and was responsible for many items that greatly aided the war effort, such as armoured trains and many items of railway engineering. He went to the USA to obtain railway equipment and to France to view the rail infrastructure there. After the war, he served on Cheshire County Council and became Mayor of Crewe during 1918 and 1919. He was a JP for Crewe and a major in the Engineer and Railway Staff Corps Royal Engineers. In early 1918 he was conferred with a CBE by the king in recognition of his services to the country during the war years. He died at Falmouth on the 18 October 1920, at the age of sixty-two. The photograph is of two footplate men relaxing in the cab of a Bowen-Cooke locomotive and the road named after him in Crewe, or rather what is left of it.

A locomotive designed by Bowen-Cooke.

The road in Crewe bearing Bowen-Cooke's name.

Coppenhall Church

St Michael's Church, Coppenhall, is a Grade II listed building, and unlike many others in Cheshire is still an active Anglican parish church. Originally a timber-framed church was on the site in around 1373 and rectors can be traced back to that date. The present church was rebuilt in 1821 and again between 1883 and 1886 to a design by James Brookes, who was a Gothic Revival architect specialising in church design. In 1880 the rector was the Revd W. Cawley Reid MA. Between 1907 and 1910 the nave was added by J. Brookes, Son & Adkins.

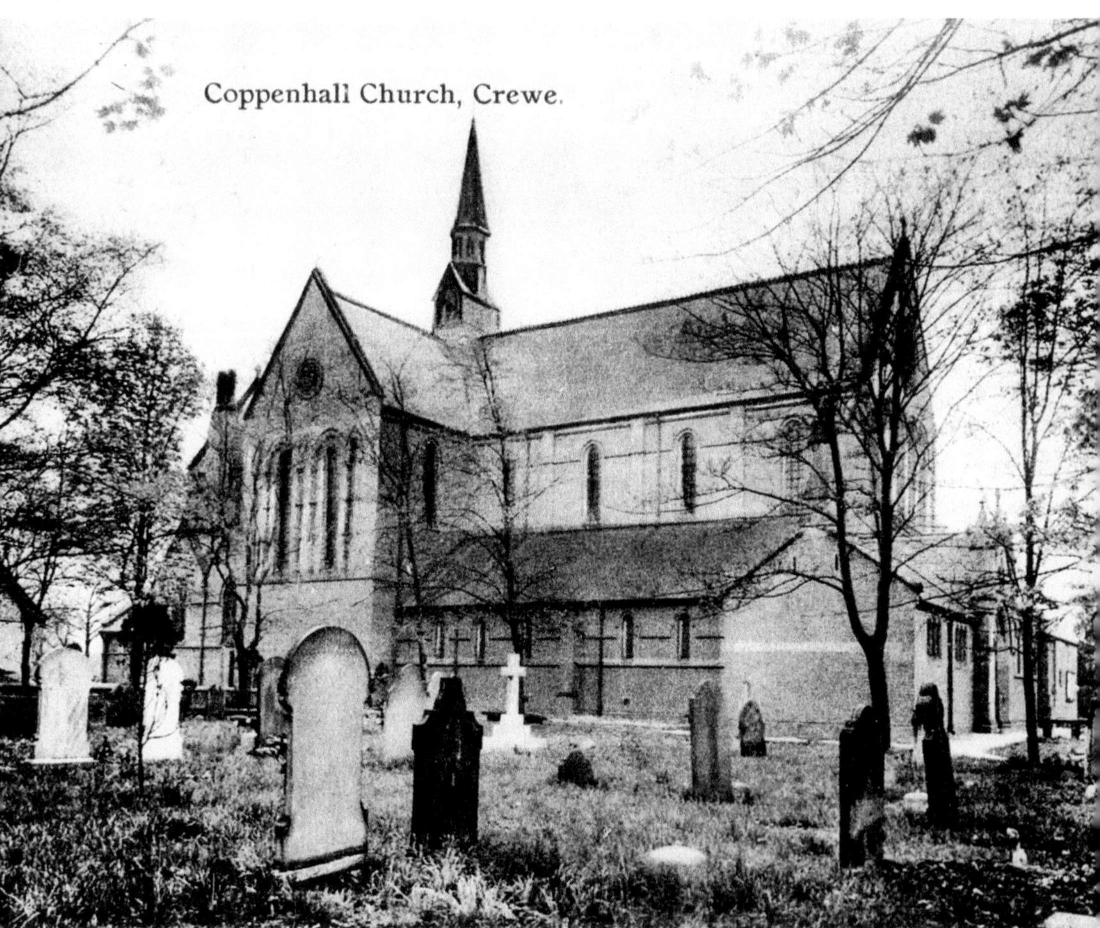

St Michael's Church, Coppenhall.

The Christadelphian Hall set back in Edleston Road.

Christadelphian Hall

Christadelphians claim to base their beliefs solely on the Bible, and their beliefs differ from some parts of mainstream Christian teaching. They are expected to read the whole of the Old Testament once a year and the New Testament twice a year. In Crewe, the sect is housed in an attractive building, set back at No. 248 Edleston Road. It is a Grade II listed building that dates to 1847 when it was a Congregational church, twenty-two years later it was converted for use as offices. In the 1930s it was taken over by the Christadelphians and returned to religious use.

Congregational Church, Hightown

The building was built in 1870 as the Congregational Chapel of the United Reformed Church at Hightown Crewe. The church itself was founded in Oak Street but rebuilt at the junction of Hightown and Flag Lane. Eventually, the congregation drifted away and the church was closed. It went through several reincarnations, a restaurant, the

The former Congregational church, Hightown, has now badly decayed.

Hightown, Crewe.

Victoria Snooker Club and then to its most recent use as a live entertainment venue called The Limelight Club. The business went into receivership in 2010 and awaits conversion to dwellings. It is, however, derelict at the time of writing, as are the buildings around it.

Christ Church Tower

Liverpool has its 'bombed out' church in the form of St Luke's in Leece Street in the city centre. The church was bombed during the war, but the tower and external walls remain and have been preserved. Crewe boasts a similar ruin in the form of the tower of Christ Church in Prince Albert Street, although this time it was not the fault of

The tower of Christ Church in 2019.

Christ Church in days gone by.

Hitler's bombers but dry rot. The church was built in 1843 by the Grand Junction Railway. It was consecrated on the 18 December 1845 by the Right Reverend John Bird Sumner, Bishop of Chester. Building work continued, and in 1877 the tower, designed by J. W. Stansby, the architect of the LNWR was built. The church served the local town centre community until 1977 when it was discovered that the building was suffering greatly from dry rot. The nave and aisles were demolished, and the diocese of Chester declared the tower and baptistry redundant on 1 June 1980. Services continued in the surviving part of the church, but these ceased in 2013. The tower and some walls remain and on the 14 June 1984, what was left of the church was listed as Grade II.

In 1878 Crewe became the scene of a minor piece of sanitary pioneering when the railway companies district estate agent invented a much-improved form of waste-water closet. He built the first one in Christ Church day schools. The apparatus was known as a 'tumbler' or 'tip-pan', and it was gradually installed in the companies many houses that were being built for the workers. By 1879 only 170 real water closets were in use in the borough. The rest were pail closets and privy middens. This was changed by the 1920 Public Health Acts that banned the further building of privies (outside toilets).

Crewe Hall

Crewe Hall was built between 1615 and 1636 for Sir Randolph (or Ranulph) Crewe, the Speaker of the House of Commons. His father was a tanner in Nantwich by the name of John Crew. Sir Randolph became the Lord Chief Justice of the King's Bench in 1625. This position only lasted until the following year when he was removed by Charles I.

He had Crewe Hall built on land previously owned by his ancestors. In fact, Crewe was the seat of the de Crewe or de Criwa family, dating back to the twelfth and thirteenth centuries when they built a timber-framed manor house on the site.

The extensive lands of the Crewe family were lost due to legal problems and came into the ownership of Sir Christopher Hatton. Sir Randolph Crewe purchased the land back from Sir Edward Coke, the husband of Elizabeth Hatton, in 1608. At the time Sir Edward was the Chief Justice of the Common Pleas and would become the Chief Justice of the King's Bench in 1613.

Crewe Hall, *c.* 1915.

The king and queen at Crewe Hall, 1913.

Right: Fireplace in Crewe Hall with plaque matching the old schoolhouse.

Below: Crewe Hall in May 2019.

At the time, the house was said to be one of the country's largest houses. It was later recorded by historian Nikolaus Pevsner to be one of the two finest Jacobean houses in Cheshire, the other one being nearby Dorfold Hall in Acton near Nantwich. In 1636 the English Civil War started, and the Crewe family were Parliamentarians. The hall was used as a garrison. Seven years later the Royalists under Lord Byron occupied the area during the Siege of Nantwich, a Parliamentary town 5 miles or 8 km away. The vicar of Acton church, from which canons were fired into Nantwich, described what happened at Crewe Hall: 'The Royalists laid siege to Crewe Hall were they, within the house slew sixty and wounded many…' The Parliamentarian's eventually won the Battle of Nantwich and soon after, Sir Randolph died and the hall passed to the Offley family through Sir Randolph's great-granddaughter Anne Crewe, who married John Offley of Madeley. The family name was resurrected in 1708 when their eldest son John took the name Crewe. Anne Crewe's great-grandson (1742–1829) was created Baron Crewe in 1806.

John Crewe had much work done on the house, as did his grandson Hungerford Crewe (1812–94). Hungerford Crewe never married, so when he died in 1894 the Baronetcy became extinct. During his occupation in 1866, there was a fire at the hall, and it was restored by E. M. Barry, the son of Sir Charles Barry, the architect of the Palace of Westminster and other notable buildings such as Highclere Castle, Charing Cross station and hotel and Great Ormond Street Hospital. One of his innovations during the restoration was the building of the West Tower. It was completed in 1870 at a cost in today's money of £14.1 million. At the time the hall doubled in size and alterations to the stables were added.

An interesting snippet is that Joseph Blumire, the coachman to John Crewe Esq in 1719, bequeathed the sum of £60. The interest was to be laid out weekly in brown bread to be distributed in the parish church at Barthomley every Sunday to the poor of Crewe township.

The hall was inherited by his nephew Robert Milnes, who adopted the name Crewe, becoming Crewe-Milnes. He became an earl in 1895 and became the Marquess of Crewe, and during his time at the hall, George V, a personal friend, and Queen Mary stayed there for three days in 1913 while touring Staffordshire. The photograph of the group around the door of Crewe Hall includes George V and Queen Mary. Robert Crewe-Milnes was in Parliament and held key cabinet positions between 1905 and 1916. He was a Liberal politician.

The Crewe-Milnes family, as happened rather often in those days, left the hall in 1922 and it remained empty until the Second World War. In 1931 the hall was offered as a gift to Cheshire County Council as the family no longer wanted to live there. However, the offer was declined, and in 1936 most of the estate was purchased by the Duchy of Lancaster.

It spent time during the war as a military camp, and in 1941 the lake was drained to prevent it being used as a visual reference for German pilots attempting to bomb the

Rolls-Royce aero engine factory. Then, from 1943, it was a prisoner of war camp for German officers and in 1947 the hall was leased to Calmic Ltd, who produced hygiene and medical products. Some 800 employees worked there. In 1955 the Queen and Prince Philip visited the hall.

Calmic was purchased by the Wellcome Foundation in 1965, and it became their headquarters in the UK and Ireland until they merged with Glaxo in 1995. In 1994 the Duchy of Lancaster sold the adjacent business site and the hall and buildings. The site became the Crewe Hall Enterprise Park.

In 1998 the hall was sold to a hotel developer, and after extension and modernisation, it became what it is today, an exclusive hotel in extensive grounds. At its centre is the beautiful Grade I listed hall. Note the photograph showing the feature above one of the fireplaces. This is a copy of the one that will be mentioned later as being on the front with glass protection at the Old Schoolhouse. It just does not bear the words 'Time rewarding industry and punishing sloth'.

Crewe Hall Stables

As well as boasting a beautiful hall, the outbuildings attached to it were something special. Here we have the stables. They were built around 1636 as part of the quadrangle on the east face of the hall. Beautiful though they were when built, they were given the addition of a tower and clock face in 1837. Edward Bloor was engaged by Hungerford Crewe, the third Baron Crewe to work on Crewe Hall. Part of the brief was to make alterations to the stable block, which he did with a new entrance in the form of a stone archway with a balcony above the tower and clock. Edward Bloor also remodelled Buckingham Palace for Queen Victoria and Prince Albert and carried out many commissions at home and abroad.

Crewe Hall stables from the front.

The rear of Crewe Hall stables.

Crewe Arms Hotel

Here we have another world first in Crewe: the first ever railway hotel. It was built in 1830 to serve the very early days of the railways.

On the front elevation is shown the date of 1880, which may be the modernisation date, but not the build date. It was built in 1830, and in 1850 it was The Crewe Arms Hotel and Refreshment Rooms with William Edwards as the manager, but, it was built by the railway company at the time when the old Crewe station was modernised. As such it is arguably the first dedicated railway hotel built in Britain. The end of the building abuts one of the platforms, and a door is set in the wall to allow exit or entry straight on to the platform. At such a location, it is obvious that many celebrities and VIPs have passed through the hotel, the most famous one being Queen Victoria. A tunnel was provided for her to pass from the station to the hotel conspicuously. It is now blocked up at either end.

The Crewe Arms Hotel, Nantwich Road.

Crompton's Clothing Factory, Bridle Road

In around 1854 the LNWR undertook the job of providing a factory for John Crompton, who produced the company's uniforms. It must be remembered that in those early days of this new transport system, the railway companies manufactured everything themselves. Railway engines, lines, uniforms, wheelbarrows, ashtrays, they were totally self-sufficient. In this case, building the factory for private enterprise to provide the uniforms. Compton's went on to make uniforms for other organisations such as the police. As you can see, this factory was originally built to provide the staff with uniforms and was built in the same style as a saw-toothed railway shed.

One famous employee was Ada Neild Chew, who worked there from 1897 and wrote some letters to the *Crewe Chronicle* under the sobriquet A Crewe Factory Girl. Despite the anonymity, she was sacked from Compton's. The letters detailed the discrimination that women faced in the workplace. She was a suffragette and dedicated socialist who later went into local politics, and after the First World War set up a mail order drapery business.

Former Crompton's Clothing Factory, Bridle Road.

Delaney Buildings and Those Alongside

These attractive buildings were built as Crewe Teacher Training College. It was designed by the county architect H. Beswick and built in 1911. It was later Grade II listed. After opening it remained as a teaching establishment, becoming part of the Crewe and Alsager College, and is now part of the Manchester Metropolitan University. This, however, will not be for long as the university is closing and its Crewe campus is likely to be taken over by a private hospital training group. The building is situated off the roundabout at Crewe Green Road and Crewe Road, the A534.

The Delaney Buildings in what was the university campus.

The buildings next to the Delaney Buildings.

Drill Hall, Myrtle Street

A quick look at the Crewe Drill Hall, which is a Grade II listed building, that is now closed. It is a former reserve centre built with others across the country in 1937. Looking at the interior of the drill hall, it is unique and has been altered over the years, and this is one of the reasons for the Grade II listing. The drill hall consists of a two-storey administrative and domestic block to the west, a hall to the east, a separate garage and a single-storey rifle range.

Drill Halls arrived on the scene in 1859 on the formation of the Rifle Volunteer Corps, and were also known as 'drill sheds'. They are dedicated training facilities for the service volunteer units. In 1859 the government opened the invite to serve in a reserve of men with military training in the same way as the regular army. It was open

Drill Hall, Myrtle Street, Crewe.

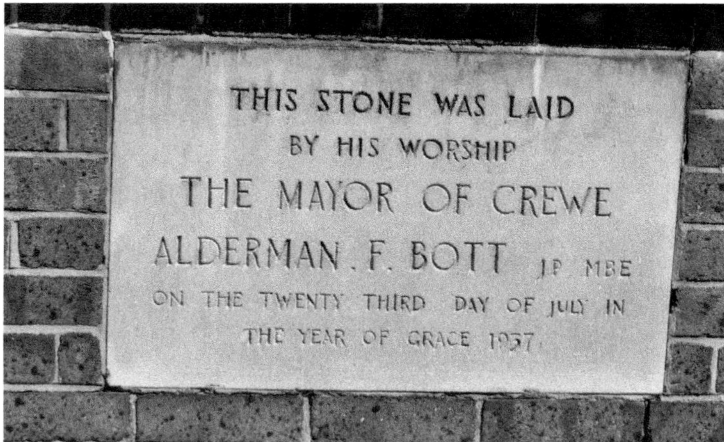

The plaque on the wall of the drill hall.

to unpaid volunteers. Within a year 120,000 had signed up and needed somewhere to train. Hence the building of dedicated drill halls and Territorial Army units, as army bases were unable to take these volunteers.

In 1937 when Crewe Drill Hall was built, a further 200 new drill halls were built around the country as the clouds of war were threatening. Crewe is unusual in being so modernistic in its appearance.

Delamere Street (No. 47)

This is the only remaining railway-designed and built house for a railway manager that remains and is a good example of one of the many managers' houses that could once be found in the area. It was built in 1850 and was designed by Joseph Locke, as were the streets and houses in the vicinity, although most have now been demolished. No. 47 Delamere Street is a Grade II listed building that once housed a manager at Crewe Railway Works. When its duties as such ended, it spent time as a convent for a small community of nuns. The Roman Catholic Church of St Mary is opposite in St Marys Street and will be mentioned later in the book. No. 47 has now been converted into student accommodation.

Ex GJR managers' house, No. 47 Delamere Street.

E

Earle Street

Earle Street was originally part of the conurbation built by the Grand Junction Railway (GJR), and before this it was named Small Lane. It was renamed Earle Street in honour of Sir Hardman Earle (1792–1877), who lived in Allerton Towers in Woolton, Liverpool (now derelict). He was a director of the Liverpool & Manchester Railway and one of the first promoters when he joined the board in 1828. Later the LNWR, before that, in 1841, he was a businessman (slave trader) and was fabulously rich. It was when Hardman Earle, on behalf of the LNWR, leased a small foundry known as the Viaduct Foundry and Engineering Company. At this time, 1853, there were just around twenty houses for the workers, but the foundry expanded, and further houses were required, and in the end this small town expanded until it had over 600 houses. The reason

Earle Street.

Modern image of Earle Street.

for leasing the foundry was because Crewe Works was running out of space and the Viaduct Foundry became the main wagon building works for the LNWR. Hardman Earle, being a director of the LNWR, was responsible for the leased foundry, and the town was named Earlstown at Newton le Willows after him. In 1860 the LNWR purchased the foundry outright, and it went from strength to strength. By 1952 under British Railways the foundry employed some 1,600 workers. Thanks to Beeching it was closed in 1964.

On 23 May 1874, Sir Hardman Earle bought Mersey Vale, a villa at No. 282 Chester Road in Hartford, near Northwich in Cheshire, for £1,600. The house is believed to be the first built and designed by the renowned architect John Douglas. Whether or not Sir Hardman ever lived there is not known, but it is unlikely. Why move there when he already lived in a huge mansion? A better guess would be that he bought it as a stopover for when he was in that area because it was right opposite Hartford station on the London to Liverpool railway line. Sir Hardman Earle probably stayed at Mersey Vale whenever he was over for the Cheshire Hunt. He was a keen follower, and there were stables for fourteen horses at the house.

F

Funsters Stalbridge Road

In 1905 a beautiful and large church in red brick was built in Stalbridge Road and went by the name St John the Baptist Church. It was originally a chapel of ease for Christ Church, Crewe, until 1914 when it became the district church for Monks Coppenhall, a parish that had been served by Christ Church and St Paul's Church. It became known as the Consolidated Chapelry of St John the Baptist. It closed in around 1994 and in 1997 what was to become a company opening dedicated children's play areas set up in the empty church in Stalbridge Road. They now have two centres serving children up to twelve years old, one Burslem and the original one here in Stalbridge Road in Crewe.

Original St John the Baptist Church, Stalbridge Road.

‘Gaffers Row’ – Victoria Street

Another one of the few remaining buildings, in this case, a row of eight terraced houses that were originally constructed for railway workers who worked as foreman. They were designed by John Cunningham for the Grand Junction Railway in 1850 and are Grade II listed. Each one was later divided into two dwellings, making 16 in number, and to facilitate this the window above the front door was bricked up. The correct address is Victoria Street, and the houses are of a better quality than the ones built for the labourers by the London & North Western Railway. The row was built from 1854 to 1856 for the foremen and their families, and a similar row was built in Delamere Street. Part of the road and houses still exist but space has been made for the entry to the bus station. The pub across the road named ‘Gaffers Row’ is closed and awaits probable demolition. I have included a photo of the old Victoria Street at the Town Centre end to show what it once looked like.

Gaffers Row, built by the railway for the foremen.

Victoria Street, Crewe, in days gone by.

Grand Junction Railway

The year 1832 was the beginning of revenue-earning railways in Britain. There were two rival companies: the Liverpool & Birmingham Railway Company and the Birmingham & Liverpool Railway Company, (now there is an example of the building frenzy that was in its earliest stages). They were amalgamated into the Grand Junction Railway and were authorised by an Act of Parliament. They commissioned Joseph Locke and George Stevenson to plan the route, although in 1835 Stevenson resigned and Locke continued alone. The route was completed on the 4 July 1837 and ran for 82 miles (132 km). The line ran from Birmingham, then travelled through Wolverhampton, Stafford, Crewe and Warrington. It then joined the Warrington & Newton Railway and then Liverpool & Manchester Railway, which had opened in 1830 at Newton Junction. The GJR over the years absorbed many smaller companies in England and Scotland, including the Warrington, Newton, Liverpool and Manchester. It eventually carried passengers from London to stations in the north. The GJR had an engineering works at Edge Hill, which they relocated to Crewe (as mentioned elsewhere) and Francis Trevithick was the locomotive superintendent. It was then under the GJR that the small village of Monks Coppenhall became part of the far bigger Crewe with its many new houses and workshops. It is fair to say that the Grand Junction Railway and the London & North Western Railway (LNWR) that it became part of later can truly be called the builders of Crewe.

Old photo of the GJR railway at Crewe.

Hack Green

Hack Green, also known as the Hack Green Nuclear Bunker and the Secret Bunker, is now a visitor attraction. The images perhaps do not show much, but this is an underground facility and is well worth a visit. It isn't in Crewe itself but is very close by and protected Crewe with its aircraft engine factory and railways throughout the Second World War. It also has a very interesting story to tell.

At the start of the Second World War, radar was in its infancy and had difficulty in detecting hostile aircraft. In late 1940 a system of radar installations known as 'Ground Controlled Intercept Stations' was developed, and in 1941 Hack Green, a site previously used as a bombing decoy site for the main railway centre at Crewe, was chosen. It became RAF Hack Green, which provided early warnings of airborne attack between Birmingham and Liverpool.

Thus began the service of Hack Green and its airmen and women in defence of the nation. The Crewe railway facilities were a target for the Luftwaffe, as was the Bentley factory. It was built just before the war for the manufacture of Rolls-Royce aero engines, which were fitted in RAF fighters and bombers. So the connection with

How Hack Green looks above ground.

An original sign from the old RAF base.

Hack Green and Crewe is a close one, albeit that it is somewhat out of the town near the village of Baddington.

Following the Second World War, a major examination of radar capability revealed that our existing radar defence would be unable to cope with the threat posed by fast jet aircraft, let alone nuclear missiles. Any operational station needed to be protected against the new threat posed by nuclear weapons. RAF Hack Green had a complement of eighteen officers, twenty-four NCOs and 224 other ranks, so quite a substantial installation is hidden away in pastoral Cheshire. The station was closed in 1966, its role having been transferred to RAF Lindholme in South Yorkshire. The bunker was then abandoned.

In the 1970s, to present a credible civil defence structure, secret plans were drawn up to ensure that should war have broken out the government would survive to lead and reconstruct post-war Britain. From the ashes of a thermo-nuclear conflict, the UK was split into eleven defence regions, each with a Regional Government Headquarters (RGHQ) protected to a high standard against the effects of nuclear weapons.

In 1976 the abandoned site at Hack Green was purchased from the MOD by the Home Office Emergency Planning Division to be transformed into a protected seat of government. The original radar bunker was converted into a vast underground complex containing its own generating plant, air conditioning and life support, nuclear fallout filter rooms, communications, emergency water supply and all the support services that would be required to enable the 135 personnel to survive a sustained nuclear attack.

So apart from the beautiful countryside in which it stands, meandering canals and the River Weaver gently lapping against its banks, what is of general interest in this quietly unassuming area of natural beauty? Well if, during the cold war in the 1980s, the Soviets had hurled a nuclear bomb at these pleasant shores 135 civil servants and military personnel would have moved into the area and taken over all the duties of a regional Government covering from the Midlands to Cumbria. The fact that it was a Regional Government Headquarters was known to a select few. To the locals, it was that old concrete bunker that used to be RAF Hack Green, the radar base. Now, it is open to the public as one of Cheshire's most popular visitor attractions.

Heritage Centre

As the most famous railway town in Great Britain and probably the world, it is only fair that Crewe has a heritage centre based around all things railway.

Crewe Heritage Centre's main entrance.

Crewe Heritage Centre.

It was built on the site of the works that were known as 'the old works', which were closed and demolished in the early 1980s. It was built to commemorate 150 years since the inauguration of the new railway town of Crewe. In 1987, Her Majesty the Queen performed the opening ceremony. The site also includes three miniature railways with 3.5 inch, 5 and 7.2 inch gauges It received the new name Crewe Railway Age in 1992. This name lasted until 2008 when it returned to the title Crewe Heritage Centre. It is located in the yard that was once part of the GJR Works and is operated by the supporters of the facility. It is open to the public every weekend between Easter and the end of September and has displays of an assortment of railway artefacts including steam, electric and diesel locomotives and has occasional guest appearances of preserved stock from the main line.

Heritage Centre's APT Advanced Passenger Train

On display on the track alongside the West Coast Main Line is one of the only remaining examples of the abandoned APT project.

The decision to design and build an APT was made in January 1969, and the first thing that needed to be acquired was funding for the project, which proved difficult. The already hard-up British Railways Board could not afford it. The Tokyo-Osaka train in Japan carried 120 million passengers a year and BRs busiest line, the West Coast Main Line, had just 6 million so not every participant felt that a lot could be spent on the new train. The Ministry of Transport was approached, and finally, in 1971, it was agreed that BR would pay half and the Ministry of Transport the other half. What was required was a train, powered by overhead electrics, that could travel

The Advanced Passenger Train that was never advanced!

at least 155 mph, cornering 40 per cent faster than expresses of the period. The project commenced, and many problems arose. The plan to put the engine in the middle of the train to equalise the weight meant that there was no link between the front and rear carriages, needing two buffet cars and staff. Empire building detracted from the work and BR, together with other agencies, were getting a bit fed up.

The idea that the best train would be multiple units with power cars at each end was still the favourite with the engines placed out of the way underneath the carriages. This was not new: the smaller diesel and electric railcars worked the same way, as did tramcars and the Blue Pullman. Work started on this interim plan and from it was born the far more successful InterCity 125, also known as the High-Speed Train or HST.

Work on the APT still limped along with long delays in construction and planning. For instance, it was discovered that two APTs passing each other from opposite directions on a bend were likely to connect as both leaned towards each other. In 1980 the APT team was disbanded, leaving onward work for other agencies. At this time the project had been running for ten years with no train yet in service. Pressure came from all sides, and eventually the government demanded that this 'money pit' be put into service, despite the ongoing problems. On 7 December 1981, the press were invited to ride on the train from Glasgow to London during which a record of four hours fifteen minutes was set. The press was not interested as they were too busy enduring a sensation similar to seasickness as the train rolled around the bends. They were not happy, although the free food and drink probably contributed to the queasiness. The train became a laughing stock as, among other things, a 'queasy rider'. Finally, the APT-P trains went into service in mid-1984, bearing in mind that the InterCity 125s had entered service in 1976 and were a great success. They were diesel and although fast at 125 mph, they were slow enough to travel virtually anywhere on the network.

By 1985/6 the APTs were withdrawn, broken up or sent to museums. One of these is the star turn at the Crewe Heritage Centre, and another is at 'Locomotion', the National Rail Museum at Shildon.

There was still a need, however, for new high-speed locomotives and upgraded infrastructure to take them. In early 1990 work started on what was to be an InterCity 250, consisting of a class 93 electric locomotive, nine coaches and a driving van trailer (DVT). In 1992 the project was cancelled due to the coming privatisation and a shortage of funding. Later came the Pendolino with Fiat Ferroviarias tilting ability. That, like the InterCity 125 and the later trains also powered by DVTs, is a success story.

Hunters Lodge Hotel

The Hunters Lodge Hotel in the Sydney area of Crewe is now a first-class and substantial hotel set in 16 acres. It started life as a farmhouse in the eighteenth century and is now a superb hotel with fifty-seven en suite bedrooms and the many other facilities commensurate with a quality hotel, restaurant and bar.

It does, however, have a dark, criminal past, so let us have a look at the rather sordid period in the life of the Hunters Lodge and to do so we have to go back to 1979. As the good townsfolk of Crewe were living their lives as normal, the owner of the Hunters Lodge, Mr Frank Edward Terpil, was in New York about to have his nefarious actions discovered, resulting a long time in prison. This gentleman had been described as one of the most dangerous men in the world.

The Hunters Lodge Hotel's main entrance.

The Hunters Lodge Hotel buildings.

Over in New York, a sting was being undertaken by two undercover detectives who had persuaded three believed gun runners that they were, in fact, Latin American revolutionaries wishing to purchase guns. They had already travelled to England to meet and convince the gun runners that they were genuine and sincere. The meeting was in the Hilton Hotel in New York, and the detectives paid the gun runners $56,000 as a deposit for a $2 million sale of 10,000 machine guns. Once the money had been handed over, the detectives declared themselves and arrested the gun runners. In the course of the continuing operation, briefcase bombs, letter bombs, grenades, poison darts, dozens of firearms and scores of documents were recovered in New York, Nutley in New Jersey and Crewe. As a result, charges were filed against two men described as major international gun runners.

Officers from New Scotland Yard and probably the SAS raided the Huntsman and arrested several people, recovering many documents. The owner of The Huntsman, Terpil had been one of the three suspects arrested in the New York Hilton sting. Frank Edward Terpil was described in court as a former agent of the Central Intelligence Agency (CIA) and had provided firearms to Libya, had trained terrorists and been an adviser to the deposed Ugandan dictator, ex-President Idi Amin. He had sold at least $3.2 million worth of weapons to the Ugandans. His co-conspirator was a George Gregary Korkala, who drove a car with diplomatic plates registered to the Ugandan Mission to the United Nations. He owned the Amstech Corporation in Nutley, New Jersey, an electronics firm from where the FBI recovered bombs, booby traps and firearms. Also arrested at the Hilton was the third man who was described as a self-confessed assassin, who became a material witness.

Terpil and Korkala were remanded in custody and faced heavy jail sentences. At the time Terpil lived in the United States, and the Ugandan Embassy confirmed that Terpil had been 'very close' to Idi Amin. Terpil also supplied the Palestine Liberation Organisation (PLO) with firearms.

The deal in the Hilton was said to promise English MK-2 and MK-3 submachine guns with the appropriate certificates to export them from England. Further enquiries by Scotland Yard determined that Terpil had purchased the Hunters Lodge Hotel in Crewe in 1978 to use as a lodge for his associates. It is believed that the British SAS were both undercover in the hotel working as staff and also took part in the raid.

Afterwards, the journalists spoke to a Sergeant Jackson at Crewe police station, and he told them that he knew nothing about the 'job', other than that there was one!

In court in the US, both were given bail. Terpil was arrested again shortly after and despite the evidence was given bail again when they both left the country! They were tried in their absence and each received fifty-three years in prison. Terpil remained free, offering his services to Yasser Arafat and Cuba. He died in Cuba in 2016 at the age of seventy-six.

I

Ice Cream Van Manufacturers – Whitby Morrison

One of the lasting memories of childhood is the sound of the ice-cream man in his multicoloured van, or in child parlance, the icey, and his well-known chimes inviting them to come to the van to partake of the treats on sale. That is if they ignore penny-pinching mum who tells them that the music means that they have no ice cream left!

So where do these child-friendly and attractive vans come from? The answer is Crewe. Whitby Morrison is the biggest ice-cream van manufacturer in the world. Bryan Whitby founded the company in January 1962 with a purpose-built factory where bespoke ice cream and associated vehicles are manufactured for a global market.

The company is still in the family. The managing director is Stuart Whitby and his three sons, Edward, who is the operations director, Kristopher, who is the production director, and Nicholas, who takes care of business development. They employ a highly

The Whitby Morrison sign.

Whitby Morrison's two new ice-cream vans.

skilled workforce of around fifty staff, ensuring that Whitby Morrison offers the finest produce and support.

The company was originally called Whitby Specialist Vehicles, then in 1989 the company changed the name to Whitby Morrison after taking over Morrison Industries of Sholing, Southampton, which manufactured ice-cream vans under the Morrisons of Southampton name at Electrofreeze Works, Botley Road.

Whenver you travel abroad and see an ice-cream van, you are more than likely to see the Whitby Morrison plaque on it. The firm operates in over sixty countries and all temperatures.

Each van is individually built on a platform of choice. Currently, the favourite is the Mercedes-Benz Sprinter, but at the request of the buyer, any suitable van base can be used.

The company sponsor a stand at Gresty Road, the home of Crewe Alexandra football team.

Ibis Styles Hotel

The Ibis Styles Hotel is an attractive modern hotel situated on Emperor Way, Crewe Business Park. The history of Crewe can be seen in the many photographs displayed throughout the public areas and in each bedroom. It is part of a modestly priced hotel chain that operates throughout Cheshire and elsewhere.

Ibis Styles Hotel, Crewe.

Imperial Hotel, Edleston Road

The Imperial Hotel is an imposing public house that dates from the 1800s and is a listed building. It is now better known as The Imperial. There will not have been much in the way of disorderly behaviour there in 1906 as the licensee was Mr A. H. Badger and next door lived the superintendent of police, Mr David Pearson.

Imperial Hotel, Edleston Road.

Isolation Diseases Hospital

Most photographs in this book are of existing buildings, but this is an exception as the buildings have been demolished. Its role in the town in the 1800s is rather important, and fortunately the need for such a hospital has now receded. The Municipal Borough Isolation Hospital for Infectious Diseases was opened by the Marquis of Crewe on 16 October 1897. It was set in an elevated position in 5 acres of land in Middlewich Street. There was a separate ward for typhoid and scarlet fever, containing sixteen beds and an isolation block for the reception of doubtful cases. It cost nearly £10,000 to build. In 1904 an additional ward for the treatment of diphtheria cases was added, containing twelve beds. It had a permanent staff. The building of the hospital in the first place did not appeal to the bean counters who wanted a smaller hospital or none at all, ignoring the soaring rates of scarlet fever and the death rates in Crewe from typhoid and scarlet fever, which in the town were considerably higher than the rest of England and Wales. Soon typhoid ceased to be a serious problem, but diphtheria was from 1890 to 1900 and onwards. The disease had become more or less an epidemic in Crewe. Tuberculosis was also a serious problem and to hopefully help the sufferers and reduce the death rate, a revolving shelter was provided in the hospital grounds. While these diseases had decreased by 1919, the most prevalent disease and the one causing most deaths from any single cause was cancer. The other hospitals, such as the Crewe Cottage hospital, also known as the Crewe Memorial Hospital in Victoria Avenue, were provided by charitable foundations, one of which was the profits from the Euston Coffee Tavern in Crewe that had been established by F. W. Webb in 1880.

Isolation Diseases Hospital, Crewe.

J

Jubilee Gardens

Situated in the Hightown area of Crewe, the gardens are in the shadow of the aforementioned former Congregational church, which became the Limelight Club. These gardens, like others across the country, appeared in Queen Victoria's Golden Jubilee year. The old postcard illustrates the park well, with the chapel in the background.

Jubilee Gardens with the former Congregation church in the distance.

(Cross) Keys

This large and attractive pub was situated in Remer Street. It was a very popular pub and actually had one of TV's Eggheads, Chris Hughes, on the pub quiz team. All of this did not stop it being pulled down to make way for more houses, a fact that led to some consternation among the locals.

The now demolished Cross Keys pub.

L

Liberal Club, Gatefield Street

This beautiful building was built in 1901 as a Liberal Club. It was designed and built in French Chateau style. In 1906 the president of the club was Mr Jas Thompson and the steward was Mr John Barlow. In 1909 when Winston Churchill was in the Liberal Party, he visited Crewe. It was during the activities of the suffragette movement, and the police had a cordon around the Town Hall. However, two women were arrested for smashing windows in the club.

The Liberal Club, Crewe.

Lyceum Theatre

Before 1881 the Lyceum Theatre in Heath Street was a disused Roman Catholic chapel that had been built in 1852 for the Irish immigrants who were working on the railways. In the meantime, a professional actor by the name of Henry Taylor was the co-founder of the society, which is now known as the Crewe Amateur Musicals Society, who had been staging shows in the Town Hall.

Then on 26 December 1881, the old church building was transformed into a purpose-built theatre called the Lyceum, and the balcony that had been part of the church was retained as the theatre's circle. At the time, music hall and stage entertainment was at its height.

In 1885 Mr Taylor and local businessmen decided that there was a need for a dedicated theatre and to this end, the Crewe Lyceum Buildings Company Ltd was founded. The running of the theatre was taken over, and plans were made to build a completely new theatre. On 21 November 1887, the New Lyceum Theatre was built on the original foundations, which consisted of 1,500 seats and was designed by the respected architect Alfred Derbyshire. Between 1906 and 1907 Charlie Chaplin, Stan Laurel and Wee Georgie Wood appeared on stage. In 1908 the theatre was renamed the New Opera House

In 1910 the theatre burnt down. According to *Crewe Guardian* reports, the fire broke out in the early hours of 11 March 1910, and within half an hour the building was a raging inferno. That evening, the audience had enjoyed the pantomime *Dick Whittington* and his cat. The fire was discovered by theatre manager Ambrose Fischer. The local fire brigade, based nearby, attended, as did the LNWR Fire Brigade. The flames could be seen in Nantwich, but the true cause was never discovered. The favoured reason was a dropped cigarette in one of the dressing rooms.

Crewe's Lyceum Theatre.

The gutted theatre was rebuilt, having been designed by Scottish architect Albert Winstanley. It was opened on 11 March 1911 and called the New Theatre.

The theatre entertained the people of Crewe and elsewhere until the 1950s, when its fortunes changed, as did the owners and management. In 1955 the theatre was bought by the Crewe Municipal Borough, and the Crewe Theatre Trust was born under Councillor James Goulding as its first chairman. In 1978 the name reverted to the Lyceum Theatre. In 1994 the theatre received a new extension and improvements to the tune of £1.5 million. The theatre was opened on the 20 November 1994 and then officially on 12 November 1996 by HRH Princess Margaret.

Leighton Hospital

The main hospital for Crewe and Nantwich is Leighton Hospital situated to the north-west of the town. It was built in 1972 and was opened by Her Majesty the Queen. The hospital was built to replace the Crewe District Memorial Hospital, the Crewe Works Hospital built by the LNER, the Linden Grange Maternity Hospital, the Coppenhall Hospital, Nantwich Cottage Hospital and the Barony Hospital at Nantwich. Accordingly, Leighton is an acute General Hospital with full A & E facilities and it comes under the auspices of the Mid Cheshire Hospitals NHS Trust. Within the facility is the BMI South Cheshire Private Hospital.

Leighton Hospital, Crewe's main hospital.

Locke, Joseph, & Railway Dutton Arches

Joseph Locke is a man whose name drifts like a thread through the history of Crewe. He was born in Sheffield on 9 August 1805 and died on 18 September 1860. George and Robert Stephenson visited the home of seventeen-year-old Joseph and his father William, an experienced mining and railway infrastructure engineer. Joseph Locke was offered a job with the Stephenson's; George Stephenson was involved in the planning of the Stockton & Darlington Railway. The Stephensons had opened a locomotive works in Newcastle upon Tyne, and Robert Stephenson was working on designing and building railway locomotives. He became great friends with Joseph Locke, a friendship that was paused in 1924 when Robert went to work in Peru for three years.

Joseph Locke worked with George Stephenson in surveying the new Liverpool & Manchester Railway. Already experienced through his father's company with surveying tunnels, Locke was asked by the directors to survey the proposed tunnel works and prepare a report for them. The subsequent report was very critical of the work already carried out under the leadership of George Stevenson, and although he remained with the firm, his relationship with George Stevenson was frosty.

In 1826 when the line was given the go-ahead, George Stephenson was appointed engineer and he, in turn, appointed the highly capable Locke as one of his assistants. Soon, the other assistant Charles Vignoles found that he could not work with Stephenson and resigned, leaving Locke as the sole assistant.

When the line was opened in 1830 eight trains were to run from Liverpool to Manchester. Stephenson was to lead in the *Northumbrian*, with Locke driving the *Rocket*. Sadly, on the journey, the MP for Liverpool, William Husskinson, was killed when he was struck by the *Rocket*. In those days, the danger of getting in the way of a locomotive was not appreciated as it was later.

Work continued on the lines in the area, and the work of George Stephenson was heavily criticised to such an extent that in 1835 his assistant Joseph Locke was made chief engineer. Locke's route avoided the need for heavy engineering work, but

Photo of Joseph Locke.

Dutton Arches, designed by Locke.

the track between the villages of Dutton and Acton Bridge required the building of the Dutton Viaduct, a brick-built viaduct with twenty arches with spans of 20 feet. Locke continued building railways across the country and abroad with great success including taking the line over Shap Fell, which was a success.

One little-known fact in all of this success was Locke's part in the building of Crewe. In 1840 when the GJR decided to move their workshops from Edge Hill to Cheshire, Joseph Locke was the engineer in chief of the GJR, and it was he who was tasked with purchasing the land from Nantwich lawyer Richard Edleston and drawing up a plan for this new railway town. There was already a small halt on the Warrington to Birmingham line and the area chosen was the small hamlet of Monks Coppenhall. Joseph Locke drew up plans for his town, and these included 220 houses, planned for middle management, skilled workmen and labourers, all laid out with various grades of superiority commensurate with the status of the person who live in them. His plans also included shops, places of entertainment, churches and works in which to build and repair locomotives, carriages and wagons. His plans were carried out by the excellent architect John Cunningham, and the completed town was described by the *Edinburgh Journal* of 1850 as 'The general appearance of Crewe is very pleasing. The streets were wide and well paved, and the houses neat and commodious.' In 1843 between 700 and 900 people, mostly from Liverpool, moved to the new houses in Crewe. Crewe UTC (University Technical College) named the Joseph Locke Building after him.

The provost of Greenock quoted: 'The name of Locke will be associated with the triumphs of the locomotive and the marvels of steam traction for all coming time.'

Three of the most important railway men died within a short while of each other: Isambard Kingdom Brunel and Robert Stephenson in 1859, and Joseph Locke in 1860. Joseph Locke can claim to be one of the most important founding fathers of Crewe town.

Mornflake Oats

Here we have a company that has existed in Crewe for many years. In fact fourteen generations of the Lea family have been milling oats in Cheshire since 1675. Morning Foods is one of the oldest companies in Great Britain and is still in the same family. The current managing director is John Lea, and Mornflake is a subsidiary. The Mornflake brand was introduced by the Lea family in 1942 during the dark days of the Second World War. Now grain from all over the UK is used in their products, and they are, as well as in the UK, exported across the world.

From *Sainsbury's Magazine*:

> John Lea, together with his sons James and Edward and nephew John Borrowdale, runs Mornflake (mornflake.com), a Cheshire-based family company that's been milling oats since the 17th century.

Main entrance to Morning Foods.

The Lea family.

Mornflake is one of Britain's oldest companies. What's its story?

When our ancestor William Lea started milling back in 1675, oats were a vital crop, powering the horses that transported goods. Hundreds of years later, we're still the same family business, still working with local farmers and still milling oats. We're also proud to be one of the few remaining independent cereal producers in Britain. The principles haven't changed, but we now mill so much more and create so many more variations. The market probably wasn't ready for granola in William Lea's day.

In 1939, my father Philip Lea wanted to join the RAF, but the government felt producing oats to feed the nation was too important. He got special permission to expand a site in Crewe, where our mill remains today. Rationing at the time meant that home-grown 'victory oats' became a staple of the British diet.

Mornflake Oats are one of the shirt sponsors for Crewe Alexander FC.

Municipal Buildings, Earle Street

This impressive building was designed by H. T. Hare and built between 1902 and 1905. It was formally opened on 19 July 1905 by the Mayor of Crewe, Alderman Arthur Griffiths Hill. After this, there was a banquet and formal reception for 140 guests, which was held nearby at the Mechanics Institute, also known as the Town Hall. The front of this attractive building features panels by sculptor Frederick E. E. Schenck (1849–1908). The building contains the Council Chamber, the Mayor's Reception Room, committee rooms and staff offices. It was once the offices of the Crewe and

The Municipal Buildings in Earle Street.

Nantwich Council but is now one of the headquarters of Cheshire East Council. In 2018 Crewe was lit up for Christmas when a spectacular light show was beamed on to the front of the Municipal Buildings.

Marmion Clothing Factory, Camm Street

In 1877 a very attractive red-brick and cream building was built for the Crewe publishing and printing company in Marmion Street. Then, in 1917, the building became a clothing factory when it was purchased by the CWS. Between 1937 and 1938 the factory was extended. It is now used for office and workshop units. It has also been a gym and sports centre for many years.

Marmion Clothing Factory, Camm Street.

Moon, Sir Richard (1814–99)

Born on the 23 February 1814 and died on 17 November 1899, Sir Richard Moon was one of the doyens of the railways. He was born in Liverpool to Richard Moon and his wife Elizabeth, daughter of William Bradley Frodsham (a Cheshire link there!). He became a member of the board of the new London & North Western Railway, an amalgam of several small lines, in 1847. He became a director and then was appointed chairman in 1861, remaining in that post until 1891.

Hightown end of Richard Moon Street.

Crewe station platform under Sir Richard Moon.

Sir Richard was in the post through those important years when the railways expanded massively, covering the whole of the United Kingdom, both successfully and not quite so successfully.

During this time, in 1869 he founded the Snowden Mountain Railway in Wales When the railway was proposed, George Assheton Smith, over whose land it would run, strongly objected as he felt it would be a blight on the landscape. Accordingly, the line was delayed for twenty years. Eventually, the line was opened from Llanberis and renamed the Snowden Mountain Railway.

The rack and pinion railway was opened on Monday 6 April 1896 in time for Moon to witness the occasion, although he died three years later. The opening ceremony was met with tragedy. As part of the celebrations, two trains left for the summit. Then on the return trip, engine No. 1 *Ladas*, with two carriages full of passengers, left the track out of control. One passenger died when he jumped from the carriage. The train was full of passengers, but that was the only fatality. The following train was not correctly informed and ran into the rear carriage, this time with no fatalities.

A later enquiry found that the accident had been caused by both the weight of the train and settlement of the newly constructed track. As a result of the accident, the train weight was decreased by reducing the number of carriages to the equivalent of one and a half carriages, and the later ones were manufactured with reduced weight allowing two carriages per train together with other mechanical innovations in safety.

During Moon's tenure as chairman from 1861 to 1891 Moon brought a great change to the once small town of Crewe. The annual receipts in 1841 were £4.3 million, and by 1891 they amounted to £11.8 million. By 1885 the company was employing 55,000 men throughout its various sites and was then the largest stock company in the world.

In February 1891, Moon's wife died, and he retired from the board of the LNWR the following month. As his son died in 1893, the Baronetcy passed to his grandson.

He is remembered in Crewe by Richard Moon Street, as seen in the photo on the side of the Technical Institute at the start of a very long road.

Market Hall, Earle Street

In 1854 when the Market Hall was built. Called the Cheese Market Hall, it was designed by Charles Meason on behalf of Mr John Hill of the Manor House, Wistaston. In 1869 it was purchased from his executors by the then Local Board. It had an edifice of brick in the Grecian-Doric style, and in 1871 the tower was added. The tower contained a four-faced clock that was presented in memory of Mr John Hill. There was a fish market and corn exchange, and in 1902 the building was under the control of Crewe Corporation.

Front of the Market Hall, Earle Street, Crewe.

Rear of the Market Hall showing old sets in the road.

Nantwich Road and the Royal Hotel

Looking now at the station end of Nantwich Road, this long and busy road stretches from the roundabout by Crewe station into the middle of Nantwich. On the way, it becomes Crewe Road and most of the way it is the A534, changing after crossing the Nantwich bypass to the B5338 into the town centre. As for the station end, with the Crewe Arms on one side of Crewe station and the Royal Hotel on the other, there has been plenty of accommodation through the years for visitors to Crewe and those staying overnight awaiting trains. In the case of the Royal Hotel, it was built in 1841 as Crewe's first post office, shortly after the Crewe Arms, and both were to serve the new method of travel – the railways. The Royal Hotel has just undergone an expensive refurbishment under new management.

Old Nantwich Road, Crewe.

The Royal Hotel, Nantwich Road.

O

Orphanage

Francis Webb started his career as a railway apprentice at Crewe Railway Works and went on to become the company's chief mechanical engineer. When he died in 1906, he left a legacy in his will to enable the building of an orphanage for the children of railway workers who died or were killed in railway accidents. This legacy was titled the Webb Orphanage Fund, and the orphanage was built on Victoria Avenue near to Queens Park. The architect was Mr J. Brooke, who based his design on the Chelsea Hospital in London. The foundation stone was laid on the 27 October 1909 by the chairman of the LNWR, Lord Stalbridge. The building was completed on 18 December 1911, and the official opening was by Lord Stalbridge's successor, Mr G. H. Claughton. The building was dedicated by the Bishop of Chester. Also included was a very attractive entrance lodge, and the matron had her own accommodation known as

An old image of the Webb Orphanage.

A more modern image of the Webb Orphanage.

West Lodge that was alongside the main building. Boys and girls were accommodated in separate wings of the home and wore uniforms. They attended West Street Infants and Junior School, and the home could accommodate twenty girls and twenty boys, but this number fluctuated.

During the First World War, the main building's east wing was given over to the military as a convalescent home for injured soldiers. The beautiful lawns were ploughed up to grow potatoes. The home was called up again in the Second World War when again the east wing was taken over by the Ministry of Health as one of the many auxiliary hospitals. After the war, the east wing continued to be used as a hospital, now under the South Cheshire Hospital Committee, until 1963.

Fortunately, safety on the railways improved greatly after the war, which resulted in far fewer orphans requiring the services of the orphanage. By the late 1950s, there were only two children in residence. On the 31 March 1961 the orphanage closed. When the use of the east wing was no longer required in 1963, the building was used by the British Transport Commission as a training centre. Then, in 1967, there was another change of direction when the Manchester NHS Trust used it as a hospital for people with personality disorders. The Webb Orphanage Fund was wound up in 2004, and the assets left from its charitable activities were passed to the Railway Benefit Fund.

The building was first listed Grade II on the 25 July 1989. It is now known as Webb House and contains twenty-four high-quality apartments.

Old Vicarage, Narrow Lane, Crewe Green

The Old Vicarage is situated on Narrow Lane, Crewe Green, and was built in 1889. It is a Grade II listed building and former vicarage that was designed by Thomas Bower in red brick. The north side of the building is dominated by a large chimney stack that contains two small windows on the ground floor. There is an inset stone panel bearing the emblems of the Crewe estate at the first-floor level. The house now is in private ownership.

Old Vicarage, Narrow Lane, Crewe Green.

(St) Paul's Church, Hightown

Crewe was an entirely new place because of the arrival of the railways and two churches were built by the railway company. The first was Christ Church in 1845 and the second was St Paul's in Hightown, which was built in 1869. At the time Francis Webb was head of Crewe Works and nominated his brother as vicar, then bullied his workers into attending the services. Three more railway churches were to be built as management tried to combat the stubborn rise of Nonconformity that was growing exponentially in Crewe and elsewhere.

As for St Paul's, it served the railway and the congregation well for many years but eventually, partly due to town planning, the congregation dwindled, and the church was put up for sale in the late 1980s.

It was purchased by Crewe Christian Concern with the intention of using it for charity. This was to develop all forms of charity work from counselling to collecting furniture for the needy. The old church still provides a service to the community and helps many less fortunate members of society.

An old photo of St Paul's Church, Hightown, Crewe.

Police Station

Here we have a photograph of Crewe police station when quite new. Crewe was quite influential at the beginning of the Cheshire Constabulary, which arrived on the scene on the 20 April 1857. It is shortly after that the police stations were built bearing the Cheshire Constabulary plaque.

However, way back in the 1500s the public relied on local communities to employ constables who would have to be attested by two or more Justices of the Peace. This gave the constables a few powers, albeit not as much as today. By the 1700s it was time for a change, and local councils were made to provide watchmen or constables who would patrol the streets at night. Rural towns and villages had to accept what was given to them in the form of protection. By 1851 there were around 13.000 policemen in England and Wales. The County and Borough Police Act was created in 1856, and the government fund police forces across the country. As a result of the Act, in the autumn of 1856 the Court of Quarter Sessions set up a special committee of Justices to establish a paid police force for each county.

In Cheshire, the first full Cheshire Police committee met at the Crewe Arms Hotel on 3 February 1857 under the chairmanship of Mr Trafford, and the Cheshire Constabulary was officially formed on 20 April 1857. The first chief Constable of Cheshire was Captain Thomas Jonnes Smith.

When I say that the Cheshire Constabulary came into being in 1857, I do not mean across Cheshire. Eventually, towns such as Macclesfield, Congleton, Stockport and city of Chester had borough forces with their own police force and chief constable, and some large towns like Birkenhead and Stalybridge already had their own force. The Cheshire Constabulary itself served the rest of the county from its HQ in Chester. In 1974 the boundaries changed, Cheshire lost and gained towns, and the borough forces were amalgamated into the Cheshire Constabulary.

The Crewe police station when new.

Queens Park, Crewe

Queens Park in Crewe is a beautiful park with extensive grounds including a lake. It is situated in Victoria Avenue, open to the public and Grade II listed. It was designed by railway engineer Frank Webb, the chief mechanical engineer of the railway company on behalf of the London & North Western Railway (LNWR). The sponsor was Sir Richard Moon, who was the chairman of the LNWR at the time.

Queens Park from above.

Queens Park's main entrance.

Old Queens Park.

Looking towards the entrance of Queens Park.

The park was officially opened on the 9 June 1888 by HRH the Duke of Cambridge in the presence of the gentry and people of Crewe.

The two lodges on either side of the gate into the park were designed by John Brooke. They were built in 1887 and the sandstone used was taken from the cutting of Lime Street station in Liverpool when it was being excavated. Both are Grade II listed buildings and have just undergone a £300,000 refurbishment to bring them up to current requirements. The lodges are not an identical pair as the West Lodge has a bell tower and was used by the chief foreman in charge of the gardeners. The East Lodge was built for the park's curator. There were only four of these, who served from 1888 to 1906.

In 2014 work started on a £6.5 million project to include a children's play area, café, bowling green and updating to the paths and bridges.

Victoria Avenue itself was quite new, having been built by the LNWR Company and declared a public thoroughfare by the Duke of Cambridge before leaving. He was driven slowly along the road in his coach to carry out the declaration.

Note the humorous addition from the time of building. On the apex of the roof on both lodges facing Victoria Avenue are two unique puns on the two people responsible for the existence of the park. On the easy lodge is a painting of a bat, moon and tree in yellow. This indicates Sir Richard Moon, chairman of the LNWR Company. On the West Lodge there is a spider's web, a tree and a spider, a play on the words of Francis William Webb, the chief mechanical engineer and the man behind the park.

The clock tower and fountain, which can be found in the entrance to the park, was paid for by donations from the employees of the LNWR Company. After the opening of the park by the Duke of Cambridge, the clock tower and fountain were unveiled by Driver Middleton of Birmingham as a jubilee memorial.

R

Ramsbottom, John (1814–97)

The father of John Ramsbottom was the owner of a steam mill in Yorkshire, and it was there that John studied and learnt all there was to know about steam engines.

In 1839 he started at Sharp, Roberts & Co. in Manchester, a firm that manufactured both static engines and railway locomotives. Charles Frederick Beyer noticed John Ramsbottom and recommended that he become locomotive superintendent of the Manchester & Birmingham Railway (M&BR). Ramsbottom took up the appointment in 1842.

Beyer was the co-founder and head of engineering at Beyer, Peacock & Co. of Gorton, Manchester, and also co-founder of the Institute of Mechanical Engineers.

Ramsbottom designed the locomotive named after himself.

In 1846 the M&BR became part of the LNWR, and in 1857 Ramsbottom became the district superintendent of the North Eastern Region. Francis Trevithick was the district superintendent of the Northern Region based at Crewe. On amalgamation, Francis Trevithick was invited to resign, and Ramsbottom moved into his office as the chief mechanical engineer at Crewe Works. While there he designed the water troughs to enable steam locomotives to pick up water on the move, and in 1852 he rebuilt LNWR 2-2-2 *Cornwall* to his own specification.

He remained at Crewe until 1871 after thirty years working for the various railway companies, but his workload did not diminish. He had been president of the Mechanics Institution in Crewe. Leaving in 1873, he founded the Owens College in Manchester, later becoming the governor. In 1883, after improving his health, he returned to the railways as consulting engineer for the Lancashire & Yorkshire Railway and as constructing engineer for the design and construction of Horwich Works. He was elected a director of the L&YR and the Beyer, Peacock & Co. works.

He died at his home 'Fernhill' at Alderley edge on the 20 May 1897, aged eighty-three.

Rolls-Royce

Originally Crewe was a tiny village that joined up with other tiny villages to make one big and important one. Then it became a world-famous railway town. Naturally, it couldn't stop there; we have already mentioned the biggest manufacturer of ice cream vehicles in the world, so now we have to look at the most prestigious motor car brand in the world.

Of course, this is Rolls-Royce. In 1884 a gentleman by the name of William Royce set up a mechanical and electrical business, and in 1904 he manufactured his first car at his factory in Manchester. This car was a two-cylinder Royce 10. While in the Midland Hotel in Manchester shortly after and by appointment, he got into a conversation with a like-minded chap by the name of the Honourable Charles Stewart Rolls, son of the 1s tBaron Llangattock of the Hendre near Monmouth. A man who had spent time at Crewe Works with the LNER but who had become a car dealer and one of the first dealers in motor cars.

Charles Rolls was so impressed with the Royce 10 car that he offered to take as many as William Royce could build, although he did say that he preferred three and four-cylinder cars. They agreed that Royce would build four models and they would be under the Rolls-Royce marque and be sold exclusively by Rolls. The Royce 10 was exhibited at the end of 1904.

Two years later a limited company was set up under the name Rolls-Royce Ltd by the founders Charles Rolls and William Royce. The world-famous company had begun trading, aided by the engineering reputation of William Royce. He already had his factory in Manchester, but the partners decided to start from scratch with a new factory in Derby. Royce designed the factory, and the first cars left the assembly line in 1908. A new six-cylinder model was designed by Royce, and it was eventually named the Silver Ghost. The company was a success, so much so that they opened another factory in the USA, but this closed in 1931 as a result of the Great Depression.

The partnership, however, did not last long. Charles Rolls was a pilot who enjoyed flying, and on the 12 July 1910 he was flying a French-Wright biplane in an air show when the tail broke off, the plane crashed, and he was killed at the age of thirty, the first person to be killed in an air crash when using a powered aeroplane. Shortly before his death and flying a fragile Wright biplane, he had been the first person to fly across the channel both there and back.

Already famous for their engines when the First World War began, RR started to manufacture engines for another quite new invention: aircraft. Already famous for the vehicles that they produced, they then became famous for aero engine production – with a wartime sideline in Rolls-Royce armoured cars too. After the war, they continued to build aero engines for both civil and military planes via another arm of the company.

Also, at the end of the war, the small car manufacturers were amalgamating into larger companies, but Rolls-Royce stayed out of it and remained independent, with one exception. In 1931 they acquired another prestigious car marque, that of Bentley Motors. Bentley had a factory at Cricklewood near London, and this was closed, the two firms working from the Rolls-Royce factory at Derby.

Old Rolls-Royce facory, now Bentley.

A Rolls-Royce car beng driven by Charles Stewart Rolls with passengers HRH the Duke of York, Lord Llangattock (Roll's father) and Sir Charles Cust.

Rolls-Royce cars were rather staid if luxurious, whereas Bentley were similar but had a more sporty appeal, so apart from the famous RR grill, the cars were very similar, with the Bentley engines tweaked slightly for speed, probably at the expense of actually being able to hear the engine noise.

During the Second World War the aero engine wing of the company stepped up to meet the needs of the RAF, providing engines, especially the RR Merlin engine, for the many types of fighters and bombers. The Derby factory was frequently bombed by the Germans during the war.

At the start of the Second World War, the government had been looking for a suitable location in which to build RR aero engines, and they decided on Crewe. The factory was built from scratch in 1938 on what was farmland. The building was completed and work started, and just five months later, the first Merlin engine rolled off the production line. During the war and at its peak in 1943 24,000 Merlin engines were produced, and 10.000 workers were employed.

After the war, aero engines continued to be built at Derby as they progressed from piston engines to jet engines. Rolls-Royce and Bentley car production moved to the aero engine factory at Crewe. In 1946 Crewe produced the first motor car, the Ivan Everden-designed Bentley Mk6. In the 1960s Rolls-Royce was crippled with debt as a result of mismanagement and the cost of developing its RB 211 jet engine. The engine itself proved a success, but by 1971 the business went into liquidation. Useful parts of the company went to the government-owned Rolls-Royce (1971) Ltd, later dropping the 1971. The core business continued, but the ownership of the car division was sold to Rolls-Royce Motors Holdings Ltd.

It was not until 1985 that Bentley sales beat Rolls-Royce sales. Rolls were aimed at the traditionally wealthy, whereas Bentley was for the wealthy businessman and the rich young. In 1980 Rolls-Royce Motor Car division was sold to Vickers plc, who sold it to Volkswagen in 1998. They, in turn, sold the Rolls-Royce brand and Spirit of Ecstasy to BMW, who built a new factory at the Goodwood estate near Chichester, West Sussex.

Ruskin High School

Ruskin High School was founded in 1902 and at that time it was known as the Crewe County Secondary School. It was not originally housed in this prestigious red-brick building but in a more cramped but equally attractive school – the Technical College in

Old photo of Ruskin High School.

Flag Lane – which is detailed later in the book. Seven years later, in 1907, the current building was built and the pupils moved into it. In 1944 the Education Act came into force and changed names again, becoming the Crewe County Grammar School. In 1978 there was another change when secondary education was reorganised, and it became the Ruskin County High School, at which time it was made fully comprehensive. In 2002 it achieved Specialist School trust status prioritising sport. In 2006 it was awarded Sports School status.

More modern photo of the high school.

S

St Mary of the Immaculate Conception Catholic Church

Situated in St Mary's Street, the Catholic church was named after the street. In 1852 the Catholic congregation worshipped in a small church in Heath Street, which was later abandoned and went on to be the first Lyceum Theatre. It had been built for the Irish immigrants who were working on the railways. After that, the upper floor in St Mary's new Catholic school was used for services until 1891 when the new

St Mary of the Immaculate Conception Church, Crewe's Catholic church.

St Mary's Church was built. It was designed by the architects Pugin and Pugin, who specialised in the design and construction of Catholic churches. The presbytery and church offices are in the next street, Gatefield Street, and the church is Grade II listed. This is arguably the busiest church in Crewe now, mainly due to the influx of Polish people who have settled in the town.

St Michael and All Angels Church, Crewe Green

This church is a Grade II building. It was built in 1857–58 and designed by the famous architect George Gilbert Scott for the 3rd Lord Crewe.

It is still an active Anglican parish church that is linked with St Mathew's at Haslington. They are attached to the diocese of Chester, the archdeaconry of Macclesfield and the deanery of Nantwich. John Ellerton was vicar at this church during his church career, who was an author who wrote the famous Hymn 'The Day Though Gavest, Lord, Is Ended'.

St Michael and All Angels Church, Crewe Green.

Station

As Crewe was at the forefront in the introduction of the railways to Britain it is only to be expected that the station is one of the most important from the very early days. It was originally opened in 1837 and is one of the most significant stations in the world. The original idea was to build it at Winsford but an earlier proposal to do this had been declined. The same applied to Nantwich due to objections from local landowners. So the small village of Church Coppenhall was chosen, a village later to be incorporated into the new railway town of Crewe. From the very beginning, the station was busy both night and day, especially in the early days when virtually everything from mail to cattle passed through. The same applies today but with slightly less traffic, especially since the post office prioritised road transport. If the HS2 project comes to Crewe, there will be changes, but the current public criticism of the project could have an effect in the future. There is a strong possibility that it will end up going the same way as the earlier APT story.

Front entrance to Crewe station.

An old platform at Crewe station.

An even older photo of a Crewe station platform.

T

Trevithick, Francis (1812–77)

The first true wheeled railway locomotive was built by Richard Trevithick in 1804. Trevithick had studied the work of William Murdoch and Nicolas-Joseph Cugnot, who had both built working models of a steam-driven road locomotive in the late 1700s. Trevithick's locomotive then became the first one in the world to haul a train along the short track at the Penydarren Ironworks in Merthyr Tydfil, South Wales. Over the next few years, attempts were made to build an engine suitable for hauling trains, but none were particularly successful, although *Salamanca*, a rack engine built by Mathew Murray for the Middleton Railway in Leeds, came close as it was able to haul a coal train. It was later destroyed when its boiler blew up!

Richard Trevithick was one of the fathers of the railways. His son Francis did not, arguably, have the skills or reputation of his father. However, he became the resident

A photo of the Francis Trevithick engine *Cornwall*.

engineer of the GJR between Birmingham and Crewe in 1840. The following year Francis Trevithick was appointed railway superintendent at Edge Hill locomotive works at a time when the works were about to be relocated to the small village of Crewe in 1843. Hence, he supervised the massive operation of transferring from Edge Hill to Crewe and the need to provide new works and housing for the workers, together with all of the other requirements in such a project. Fortunately, he was well supported by his works manager, Alexander Allan (1809–91), who carried out much of the design work. Arthur Reginald Trevithick (1838–1939), his brother, was assistant works manager at the new Crewe Works.

Francis Trevithick did have one notable locomotive to his name, and that was the design of *Cornwall*, which was built with 8-foot driving wheels for express passenger work and was soon copied. It was thought then that the bigger the driving wheels, the faster the engine would travel with less strain.

In 1846 the GJR became part of the London & North Western Railway (LNWR), and Francis became the locomotive superintendent of the Northern Division.

In 1857 the Northern and North Eastern Divisions of the LNER were combined, which were originally the Manchester & Birmingham Railway. At that time the locomotive superintendent of the North Eastern Division was John Ramsbottom. Francis Trevithick was locomotive superintendent of the Northern Division, and as only one superintendent was required, he was ordered to resign, with John Ramsbottom taking over at Crewe.

Richard Trevithick moved to Cornwall where his grandfather had been a mineral agent during the 1700s, and Richard became factor of the Trehiddy estates. He wrote his father's biography, had it published and died in Penzance on 28 October 1877.

Technical Institute, Flag Lane

This highly attractive building was built as the Technical Institute in 1897 to the design of James Stevens of Manchester and Macclesfield for the Technical Institute Committee. It was built in the English Renaissance style in 1896 by A. & E. Hulse of Winsford in red brick with beautiful terracotta panels to a very high standard, forming the words Technical Institute. It was formally opened on Saturday 16 October 1897 by the Earl of Crewe in the presence of the mayor, Alderman W McNeil. During the building, a council suite was incorporated, and in 1906 the town council would meet here regularly.

Richard William Bailey was born in Romford on 6 January 1885 and died in 1957. Initially, he worked at Stratford Locomotive Works as an apprentice, and later he worked on the electrification of the suburban lines around London. Then with few chances of promotion with the Great Eastern, Bailey became a lecturer at Battersea Polytechnic and then became the principal of the Technical Institute at Crewe.

An old photo of the Technical Institute.

A 2019 photo of the Technical Institute.

There, in 1919, he became friends with Henry Guy, who urged him to join British Westinghouse, later to become Metropolitan Vickers, where he was a senior member of the research team. A notable project was the Turbomotive locomotive that later became a conventional steam locomotive named *Princess Anne* and that sadly crashed in the Harrow and Wealdstone rail disaster. He also became involved with the design of the jet engine for aircraft. He later became the president of the Institute of Mechanical Engineers in 1954. As for the building, it was Crewe Technical College for a while but has now been sold and converted into dwellings.

Timpson, Anthony Edward

Anthony Edward Timpson was born in Knutsford on 26 December 1973. His father John is the CEO and owner of the nationwide chain of Timpson shoe repair and key cutting shops, including the one shown here in Crewe. Anthony had a brother and sister, and they shared their upbringing over the years with the eighty children that his parents fostered. The firm has been in the family for five generations and they have 550 shops. In the by-election of 2008, after the death of Gwyneth Dunwoody MP, Edward was elected MP for Crewe and Nantwich. He was re-elected in the 2010 election and became the Parliamentary Private Secretary to Theresa May, the Home Secretary. In September 2012 he was appointed Minister of State for Children and Families. Then, in the 2017 election, he lost his seat to Laura Smith by just forty-five votes.

Timpson's shop in Crewe.

Union Street Baptist Church

Here is another building provided by the railway company for the benefit of the railway workers and the people of Crewe. The church was designed by J. Wallis Champion, and it was built in Union Street between 1882 and 1884. It became a Grade II listed building in 1999. At the time of writing, the church is awaiting a new minister.

Union Street Baptist Church.

Above: Ursuline Convent and School, Nantwich Road, 2019.

Left: Ursuline Convent and School, Nantwich Road.

Ursuline Convent and School, Nantwich Road

This building dates from caround 1910 and was designed by Philip Webb. It was built as an convent for a French order of nuns from the Ursuline Order. In the second half of the twentieth century it became a police training college and vehicle maintenance facility for the Cheshire Constabulary. A residential extension was erected for the students and vehicle maintenance workshops. It was at the training centre that officers received their first insight into police work, then later courses throughout their career. Courses were run in all aspects: CID, Traffic and all of the sub-branches. When the new police headquarters was built in Winsford during 2002 the college and maintenance centre was transferred there. The old convent was closed and the new extension, etc., demolished. The main building was converted into apartments and houses were built in the grounds.

V

Village School, Crewe Green

This building was built in 1882, mainly for the children whose parents were employed by the Crewe Hall estate. Since closing as a school, it has been used for other purposes and is now the church hall for nearby St Michael and All Angels Church. Apart from being a beautiful Grade II listed building, it is also quite famous for the decorations that adorn the exterior walls. The first is a plaster cast bas relief, protected by a glass screen, of a large winged male berating lounging figures, and it bears the verse 'Time rewarding industry and punishing sloth'. This is logged in the Conway Library of the Courtauld Institute of Art in London. There is also a similar alabaster figure set in one of the fireplaces within Crewe Hall but without the wording.

Above this carving on the church hall is the emblem of the Crewe estate and the words 'What shall we render unto the Lord'.

One-time village school in Crewe Green.

Plaque on the wall of the old village school.

War Memorial

Crewe already had a memorial to the servicemen who died in the Boar War, which is situated in Queens Park. The 700 servicemen who died in the First World War were deserving of a memorial, and as Crewe was a railway town, initial negotiations were made with the LNWR with regards to a joint memorial in Crewe. This was declined as

Crewe War Memorial in the Municipal Square.

the company already had a memorial to their dead in Euston station. The decision was made to erect a memorial in the Market Square, and seven models were submitted as proposals. The committee decided to have the one proposed by Walter Gilbert built, and in 1922 it was erected and consists of a sculpture of Britannia standing on a pedestal. The sculpture was cast in bronze by H. H. Martin & Co. of Cheltenham. Surrounding it are bronze panels bearing the names of the service and ranks of those Crewe service personnel who lost their lives in the two wars. On the 14 June 1924, the statue was unveiled by General Sir Ian Hamilton and the memorial dedicated by the Bishop of Chester. In 2005 it was taken down and conveyed to the National Conservation Centre in Liverpool for restoration. It was returned and installed in Municipal Square in 2006.

Francis Webb, Mayor of Crewe.

Webb, Francis (1836–1906)

Francis William Webb was born at Tixall Rectory in Staffordshire where his father was rector. On 11 August 1851, at the age of fifteen, he was articled as a pupil of Francis Trevithick at Crewe Works. At the end of his training in 1856, he joined the drawing office at the works. Three years later he became chief draughtsman, and in 1861 he was appointed works manager at Crewe and chief assistant to John Ramsbottom. In 1866 he resigned from Crewe Works and went to work at the Bolton Iron and Steel Works. It's believed that he did so to gain experience of steel making as this had just started at Crewe Works. The works manager, in his absence, was Thomas Stubbs. In 1870 Webb gave a year's notice at the steel company. Soon after this Thomas Stubbs died suddenly, aged thirty-four. He would have been preparing to become Ramsbottom's predecessor. Richard Moon, the chairman of the LNWR, contacted Webb and invited him to return to Crewe as locomotive superintendent. On 1 October 1871, he took up the position at Crewe. Within a very short time of him taking up the new role, the title of locomotive superintendent was changed to chief mechanical engineer, and that is what he became. He remained CME of the LNWR until 1 July 1903, tendering his resignation in November 1902, giving twelve months' notice. His successor George Whale was appointed to the role in April 1903 but took up the role slightly earlier as Webb became seriously ill in June. Webb died on 4 June 1906 in Bournemouth, aged seventy. During his time as CME, a vast number and class of locomotives were built

Webb's *Hardwicke* locomotive.

at Crewe. Most were excellent, but a few were not and attracted criticism from railway companies and drivers.

He was a philanthropic man who took up civil duties in Crewe. He was an alderman in the Crewe Town Council and Mayor of Crewe twice. He was vice-chairman of the Institute of Mechanical Engineers and the Institution of Civil Engineers. He was behind the building of Queens Park, and, with the chairman of the LNER Richard Moon, he presented the park to Crewe Corporation. A road in Crewe called Frank Webb Avenue is a tribute to this great man.

Whale, George (1842–1910)

A railway engineer who started from the bottom and worked his way up to locomotive superintendent at Crewe Works, George Whale was born in Bocking, Essex, and started work in 1858 as an apprentice at Wolverton Works. When the LNWR management decided, in 1862, that it would concentrate on locomotive building and repair at Crewe Works, he was one of 400 workers who was transferred there from

George Whale-designed locomotive *City of Liverpool.*

Wolverton Works. In 1865 he started work in the drawing office and in 1867 he joined the Running Department of the LNWR. Thirty-one years later, in 1898, he became responsible for the running of all LNWR locomotives.

Francis Webb was the chief mechanical engineer and was due to retire at the end of July 1903, but he became seriously ill. George Whale had already been nominated as the next chief mechanical engineer, so he stepped in to carry out the duties in full, taking up the role in April 1903.

Although Webb had many good points and had been behind the manufacture of many classes of locomotive, some were not well received, such as his compound locomotives. George Whale hit the ground running, and in a very short time rebuilds of the compounds to simple-expansion locomotives had started, and within nine months completely new classes had been designed. His 4-4-0 Precursor Class was well received, and it was quickly followed by his 4-6-0 Experiment Class. Between 1904 and 1909 he was responsible for the development of 455 locomotives. The final sixty that he ordered were ordered by Whale but delivered after his retirement by the next chief mechanical engineer C. J. Bowen-Cooke. Whale was to retire at the end of 1908, and on 1 March 1909, Bowen-Cooke became the CME. George Whale died at Hove, Sussex, in March 1910, aged sixty-seven.

X Academy, South Cheshire College

Situated in a custom dance studio within the South Cheshire College is the X Academy. If you're looking for a fun, family-run dance school in your area, then look no further. Whether you're looking to train intensively and take dance as a career or you're just looking for fun and fitness, X-Academy School of Performing Arts is the place to be. It is located at the South Cheshire College. The school delivers classes from three beautifully mirrored and air-conditioned dance studios. Classes are available for children three years plus and adults of all abilities. In some genres, classes are held specifically for boys. Ballet, tap and modern (theatre) are taught to ISTD (the Imperial Society of Teachers of Dancing) syllabi. Graded exams are available in these for students wishing to take them. Students not wanting to take the exams can still fully take part in the classes.

In addition to this studio space, the college facilities also include a large indoor theatre, as well as an outdoor amphitheatre.

Y

YMCA, Nos 189–197 Gresty Road

This building was built in the days of steam when engine crews would need accommodation for the nights that they were away from home. In 1897 the railway company built one such building at Nos 189–197 Gresty Road, which provided for the crews ending their shift in the south sheds. There was another in Mill Street covering the north sheds. These large barracks were functional buildings: there were beds for the crews and canteen and dining room facilities. The Gresty Road hostel is now a YMCA Hostel. It has recently had a multimillion-pound investment, providing extensive and modern facilities within the attractive old structure.

Old enginemen's barracks, Gresty Road, now the YMCA.

Zoo

Lakemore is a family-run farm park that opened twenty years ago when Tony Ashmore decided to welcome the public into his family farm.

It is now run by the next generation of the family, who operate the park as a working farm that is open to the public. Since taking over the farm fifteen years ago, the Lewis family have worked to ensure the public can experience the true reality of a farming environment. Their vision is to ensure the farm is accessible to all children, with the

Lakemore Farm and Petting Zoo.

Lakemore Farm and Petting Zoo.

aim being to provide them with their first experience of animals and the countryside. The farm is also home to Cattlearch Livestock, an award-winning group of pedigree animals including Limousin cattle and Texel sheep, which visitors can get close to, pet and feed. There is an onsite lakeside coffee shop together with indoor and outdoor picnic areas, and an indoor play barn with soft play, outdoor park and crazy golf, which are ideal for younger children. Visit www.lakemorefarm.com for more details.

About the Author

Paul Hurley is a writer, author and a member of the Society of Authors. He has contributed to railway and other magazines, written an award-winning novel, two large format railway books and twenty-nine local history books. He is married to Rose and has two sons and two daughters. He lives in Winsford, Cheshire.

Books by the same author:

Fiction
Britain Invaded

Non-Fiction
Middlewich (with Brian Curzon)
Northwich Through Time
Winsford Through Time
Villages of Mid Cheshire Through Time
Frodsham and Helsby Through Time
Nantwich Through Time
Chester Through Time (with Len Morgan)
Middlewich & Holmes Chapel Through Time
Sandbach, Wheelock & District Through Time
Knutsford Through Time
Macclesfield Through Time
Cheshire Through Time
Northwich Winsford & Middlewich Through Time
Chester in the 1950s
Chester in the 1960s
Chester Pubs (with Len Morgan)
Northwich Through the Ages
History Tour of Chester
History Tour of Macclesfield
History Tour of Knutsford
History Tour of Nantwich
History Tour of Northwich
Steam Nostalgia in the North of England (with Phil Braithwaite)
Remembering Steam with (Phil Braithwaite)
The Changing Railways of Britain (with Phil Braithwaite)
Cheshire with Historic England